"A tool to jumpstart ministry, evangelism, witness, and service. We all can begin to be faithful disciples right where we are — in our homes, work, and communities. With member mission, we stand a good chance of capturing the spark and vision that energized the early church in its rapid growth and mission. Highly recommended!"
– The Rt. Rev. Joe G. Burnett, Bishop, The Episcopal Diocese of Nebraska

"Using this book, I came to realize that I, as an individual, a lay person, in my daily life could spread the love and glory of God in places that could not be readily reached by the church. I now share the Good News wherever I am every day."
– Randy Rogers, Lay Leader, Cutchogue United Methodist Church, Cutchogue, New York

"Releases ordinary people, in ordinary life experience, from bondage — the notion that mission takes them out of their 'normal life' to some other 'place.' The book invites us to get serious about mission where we all actually live: in our homes, our neighborhoods, our workplaces, places of leisure, and the wider world. Now in a pronounced economic recession, I find people need this freedom to join Jesus in his battle with evil and death more than ever!"
– The Rev. Jonathan B. Coffey, Rector, St. Mark's Episcopal Church, Jacksonville, Florida

"A blueprint for engaging individuals, small groups, or whole communities in a better understanding of mission. The book identifies the multitude of arenas where the mission of the church actually occurs."
– Anne M. Watkins, Member Mission Leadership Trainer and Parish and Ministry Development Consultant, Norwalk, Connecticut

"Appreciated! The concepts and practical, hands-on tools. Invaluable!"
– Andrew Hersh-Tudor, Member Mission Leadership Trainer and Library Director, Wenatchee Valley College, Wenatchee, Washington

Living the Gospel

A Guide for Individuals and Small Groups

A. Wayne Schwab
and Elizabeth S. Hall

Library of Congress Cataloging-in-Publication Data

Schwab, A. Wayne.
   Living the Gospel: a guide for individuals and small groups / A. Wayne Schwab and Elizabeth S. Hall.
     p. cm.
   ISBN 0-9717552-1-3 (alk. paper)
1. Christian life—Textbooks. I. Hall, Elizabeth S. (Elizabeth Schwab), 1962- II. Title.
   BV4511.S39 2010
   248—dc22
                        2010034050

Living the Gospel: A Guide for Individuals and Small Groups

First Member Mission Press Edition 2010, Hinesburg, VT 05461

Copyright © 2010 A. Wayne Schwab

All rights reserved. Printed in the United States of America. For permission to reprint excerpts contact: Permissions, Member Mission Press, P.O. Box 494, Hinesburg, VT 05461 or membermission@aol.com. To reprint other material, write directly to the publisher or holder of the copyright. Sections of the book may be excerpted or copied for noncommercial purposes, including training and educational activities of congregations.

Cover and book design by Media Graphics, Inc.

Copies may be ordered from:

Member Mission Press
P.O. Box 494
Hinesburg, VT 05461

membermission@aol.com

www.membermission.org

CONTENTS

Our Vision vii

Introduction 1

    A new look at being a Christian 1

    Mission and missionary: a rethinking 2

    Love and justice: the signs of God's presence and work 3

    The Gospel and salvation 4

    A theology for member mission: seven truths 5

SECTION I: How to Use this Guide 7

    Supplies 7

    Meeting guidelines for small groups 8

    Suggestions for group leaders 8

    Oral method 9

    Rapid written method 9

SECTION II: Six Activities to Discover and to Carry Out Your Daily Missions 11

    Leader's guidelines for Section II 11

    Beginning the discovery 15

    Activity 1: What I am doing right now to make the world a better place 16

        Leader's guidelines 16

    Activity 2: Discerning my daily missions 18

        Leader's guidelines 18

        Notes for sharing worksheets 23

    Activity 3: My daily missions at a glance 24

        Leader's guidelines 24

    Activity 4: My road map for my daily missions 26

        Leader's guidelines 26

    Activity 5: Discovering God's gifts for my missions 28

        Leader's guidelines 28

    Activity 6: Finding a teammate 30

        Leader's guidelines 30

SECTION III: Making Decisions and Moving Ahead 35

SECTION IV: Worksheets, Examples, Tables, and Resources .. 37

Worksheets

Activity 1: Worksheet: What I am doing right now to make the world a better place 38

Activity 2: Worksheet 1 for discerning my daily missions – Home 39

Activity 2: Worksheet 2 for discerning my daily missions – Work 40

Activity 2: Worksheet 3 for discerning my daily missions – Community 41

Activity 2: Worksheet 4 for discerning my daily missions – Wider world 42

Activity 2: Worksheet 5 for discerning my daily missions – Leisure 43

Activity 2: Worksheet 6 for discerning my daily missions – Spiritual health.................... 44

Activity 2: Worksheet 7 for discerning my daily missions – Church life and outreach...... 45

Activity 3: Worksheet – My daily missions at a glance 46

Activity 4: Worksheet – My road map for my daily missions...47

Activity 6: Worksheets – Finding a teammate 48

Examples

Example A: Jim's and Margaret's missions on a specific day 13

Example B: Hints and sample responses for the home and work mission fields 19

Example C: My daily missions at a glance – two sample columns 25

Example D: Sample road map for my home and work mission fields..............................27

Example E: Finding a teammate at work 32

Example F: Finding a teammate – stories.. 33

Example G: A completed glance chart and road map 53

Tables

Table 1: The fields of daily life 15

Table 2: Enhancing responses to Activity 2 worksheets.. 23

Table 3: God's gifts to us.. 29

Table 4: A guide for Christian decision making 35

Resources

Resource A: Our fields of daily life are our daily mission fields 56

   The grand name for Christian work 57

Resource B: Four steps to practice finding a teammate.. 58

Moving still farther ahead... 59

OUR VISION

In Jesus Christ, God is on mission everywhere all the time. That mission is to overcome evil, sin, and death and to bring the whole of creation to fulfillment in the Holy Spirit. We join God's mission in baptism. As Christians, we are on mission wherever the decisions and actions that shape life are made.

In today's world, all of the baptized – not just the ordained and the congregations they lead – are the primary agents of God's mission in Jesus Christ. God uses us to carry on God's mission to make the world a better place – more loving and more just. In each part of our daily lives – our homes, our work, our communities, the wider world, our leisure, our spiritual health, and our churches – we are in the places where the decisions that shape our lives are made, the decisions that can advance God's reign of love and justice. We are at the dinner tables, on the construction jobs, in the schools, in the boardrooms, and in the legislatures. The church – from its congregations to its worldwide bodies with their programs, resolutions, and committees – is not in these places. We, all of the baptized, are in these places. As agents of Jesus' mission, each one of us shares in Jesus' power – the power of the Holy Spirit (John 20:22) – to make the changes that are needed. Joining with others committed to love and justice, we can be part of making the changes that increase God's reign[1] on earth.

These days, we hear a lot about church growth and congregational development. Now it is time to talk about *mission growth* and *mission development*. When congregations focus on calling, forming, sending, and supporting their members as missionaries of Jesus Christ, growth and development will happen along the way to mission. This is the "member mission" vision: all members as agents of Jesus' mission to make every part of their daily lives more loving and more just; and their congregations guiding and empowering them through their common life and worship.

How do we actually live this vision? Our baptismal vows are rich descriptions of the Christian life. Yet, they do not get down to the specifics of how to live out our vows. This guide will help you as an individual or small group to discover your specific daily missions and to draw others to work with you on them. A second guide, *Living the Gospel: A Guide For Church Leaders*, will

---
[1] God's "kingdom" is a more familiar term than God's "reign." However, "kingdom" can suggest some specific place or some form of social order. The four Gospels use it to mean God's presence among us in power. When Jesus introduces a parable saying "the kingdom of God is like …," he is about to describe what life is like when God's rule or reign is obeyed. When Jesus heals a man who is mute, he says, "… the kingdom of God has come to you …" (Luke 11:20b). God's power has overcome a demonic power. In this workbook, we use God's "reign" to emphasize God's power at work among us.

help pastors and lay leaders to implement the member mission vision in their congregations. Also, resources such as *When the Members Are the Missionaries: An Extraordinary Calling for Ordinary People* (Member Mission Press, 2002), the website at www.membermission.org, the Member Mission Newsletter, and the Member Mission Network, Inc. office can help. To contact: email membermission@aol.com or visit our website at www.membermission.org.

We have designed this guide to help you with ways to discern and carry out your missions – to help you capture your sense of where God is at work and how to join with God in that work. Note that it can be used by anyone regardless of your present level of faith. It is for any Christian or for any person for whom God, love, and justice are primary. Further, this guide is designed for use by either individuals working alone or with a partner or by small groups.

As you work through this guide, have on hand a bible and a copy of *When the Members are the Missionaries* by A. Wayne Schwab, which can be purchased through www.amazon.com or email membermission@aol.com.

We have found in using this guide with individual and groups throughout the United States, it is beneficial to allow twelve weeks to complete the entire process. However, any six of the activities in Section II can be used alone or in any grouping that fits your situation.

When you have completed the activities in this guide, you can expect to be empowered by a clearer sense of what God is calling you to do in each part of your daily life and by a deeper sense of God's presence to help you to do it.

A. Wayne Schwab and Elizabeth S. Hall

September 2010

INTRODUCTION

Before working on the activities in this guide, it's important to understand some of the thinking and theology behind the vision of member mission. In this introduction, you will find:

- A new look at what it means to be a Christian in today's world.

- A redefinition of the following terms: mission, missionary, evil, love, justice, Gospel, and salvation.

- A theology for member mission.

A word of caution: this guide is about a process, not a program. Overuse of the term "member mission" can make member mission into a program or gimmick. Avoid capitalizing it and try to use other wording such as "living our missions daily" as often as possible.

A new look at being a Christian

Everyone at some point asks questions about their lives. If you are like most people, you have faced three fundamental questions:

- Do I matter?

- How can I make a difference in this world?

- How can I have a closer relationship with God?

Philosophers and theologians have wrestled with these questions since the beginning of time. What you may not know is that there are answers to these questions. Yes, there are. And these answers can guide the rest of your life. That is what this guide is all about. It's designed to help you to find the answers to those questions, find your place in the world, and do what you are uniquely called and qualified to do as part of the Lord's work on earth.

In member mission, you are the fundamental agent of change for God and your church plays a supporting role. That's because, as an institution, the church is limited in what it can do to make real and lasting change. Think about it. The church can advocate for more food stamps for the poor, but individual lawmakers have to vote for the increase. If we want to help the poor, help church going lawmakers to recognize the connection between what they hear on Sunday and do on Monday in their legislatures. When legislators make what we call the "Sunday to Monday connection," they become God's missionaries in the world as they work to care for the poor.

Taking a fresh look at our lives as Christians, we realize what a daunting task it is to be part of God's mission. How do you find out just what God expects? Should you sell the clothes off your back and move to the Third World? Is Christianity limited to what you do in church on Sunday? What about the rest of the week? You may have read books on Christian living and still don't know what to do.

Wouldn't it be great if there was some way to discover what you should be doing? And wouldn't it be wonderful if your congregation could help you to do it? What we all need are road maps made with prayer for God's guidance and that help us to see the roads ahead as we journey on as Christians. A road map shows you all the specific turns and routes to take on your journey. We will help you to make your own road map of where you sense God to be leading you in each part of your daily life – your daily missions. As we continue, you may need to rethink "mission" and "missionary."

Mission and missionary: a rethinking

Then I heard the voice of the Lord saying,

"Whom shall I send, and who will go for us?"

And I said, "Here am I; send me!"

—Isaiah 6:8

The terms "mission" and "missionary" tend to bring to mind people who have given up everything to serve the Lord in far-flung places with few resources. There is, however, a more profound way to understand these terms. You become a missionary when you respond to your sense of what God wants you to do. God gives you your mission and has a vested interest in how things turn out!

Actually, you do not have *a* mission; you have *seven*. You have a mission in each area of daily life – your home, your work, your community, the wider world, your leisure, your spiritual health, and your church. In each area, God is already at work and wants you to share in what is already being done there.

Your church can provide the guidance and help for the critical and sacred work of discerning each of your daily missions. It can prepare and support you and your fellow missionaries seven days a week, 365 days a year. Your church holds up the call to loving and just living in its teachings and communicates the power to live that way in its sacramental life – supremely in the bread and the cup of the Lord's table. What if you are not a churchgoer? If you try to live a loving and just life every day, you are already doing God's work. But why try to do this work on your own? Why not seek out the help, love, and support you need to live better every day? Find a church where you feel at home. If you are at odds with the denomination you grew up in, try a new one. Find out where people you know and respect go and go there yourself. You don't have to cover all the bases yourself. The Lord already has a team on the field and you can come to see yourself as part of it.

Keep in mind that no matter what your circumstances in life are, no matter how insignificant or lost you may feel at times, you are never without value. You are a missionary, a Christian missionary. You have critical work to do for the Lord and no one can replace you or the contribution you will make. Your missions don't end with the closing hymn on Sunday; they are just beginning.

Next, we will look at the concepts of love and justice as starting points for understanding the theology that undergirds member mission.

Love and justice: the signs of God's presence and work

> *What does the Lord require of you*
>
> *but to do justice, and to love kindness,*
>
> *and to walk humbly with your God?*
>
> —Micah 6:8

Wherever you find love and justice, God is present and at work. Wherever the two are weak or absent, that is a call to join the Lord who is already there working to restore them and to overcome evil and sin. What do these terms "evil," "sin," "love," and "justice" mean?

Here are some fresh definitions – biblically based, just restated.

- Evil is whatever blocks love and justice. Evil separates people from God and from one other.
- Sin can be understood as evil chosen consciously.
- Love occurs when, without limit, we seek to value others as they really are and to care for them, to forgive their faults, and to help them put their skills and talents to their best possible use.
- Justice is the "public" face of love. In public life, we love by seeking for everyone equal access to the good things in life – whatever helps people to become all that they are created to be and to put their skills and talents to their best possible use.

Jesus sums all this up in Matthew 22:39, "You shall love your neighbor as yourself." Behind these words lie the very same words in Leviticus 19:18, "You shall love your neighbor as yourself;" and the question of Micah 6:8, "What does the Lord require of you but to do justice, and to love kindness, and to walk humbly with your God?" Jesus, himself, is the supreme example of love and justice. To follow Jesus means to be loving in our personal relationships and to be just in our public life – to work for everyone to have equal access to the same rights and opportunities. To follow Jesus means to work for the well-being of the whole of God's creation. Love and justice open the door for a useful way to discuss two words central to mission – gospel and salvation.

The Gospel and salvation

Christianity has a unique message. God not only tells us how to live; God helps us to do it.

We are called to be loving and just in every relationship, in every part of life. Our problem is that we do not have the power to do it. We can go part of the way but not the whole way. By ourselves, we do not have the power to cope effectively with whatever blocks love and justice. We need to be helped – to be *saved* – from the powers of evil, sin, and death. Where is such a power? And can we share it?

The good news – the *Gospel* – is that the power we seek is at work in Jesus Christ and he shares that power with us.

The risen Jesus tells the disciples to continue his work, "As the Father has sent me, so I send you" (John 20:21b). The Father sent him to make clear that God's power overcomes evil, sin, and death. Jesus has that power and shares that power – the Holy Spirit – with us. "He breathed on them and said to them, 'Receive the Holy Spirit'" (John 20:22). Here is the help – the *salvation* – we need. We share Jesus' power – the Holy Spirit – to love and to be just. We have the power, with Jesus' help, to act and to act with confidence. The same Holy Spirit that Jesus breathed on his disciples two thousand years ago he also breathes on us. Therefore, with courage, we can act and can seek to do what we believe God calls us to do.

Our baptism and reaffirmation of faith are our commitment to join Jesus to make the world more loving and more just.

As you move forward in your journey of self-discovery, keep in mind the seven truths that are a theology for member mission on the next page. Copy this list for your own frequent reference and for all with whom you work.

A theology for member mission: seven truths

Member mission is based on seven truths about God and the relationship we share with God. Our thinking and actions as missionaries are based on these truths.

1. God is always on mission. God is always working with and through us to make the world more loving and just. Teachers helping children learn to read, aid workers distributing food to the hungry, and people reaching out to others in time of need are all signs of God's mission. Wherever you find love and justice, God is at work.

2. God's mission has a church. The church does not have a mission. Rather, God's mission has a church. The church is the visible instrument of God's mission. The church collaborates with any person or group working for greater love and justice.

3. God wants us to share in God's mission every day. On Sunday, many of us work in "congregational missions:" participating in the altar guild, leading and teaching church groups, or operating a soup kitchen. "Member missions" are what church members do daily at home, at work, in their communities, in the wider world, and in their leisure to make life more loving and more just. They can vary from rebuilding a broken relationship with a loved one to voter registration to working for more just pay for employees. Member missions take us to the places where congregational missions cannot go to make the kind of real changes that only committed individuals in those places can make. Therefore, we believe that God cares as much about what we do from Monday to Saturday as what we do on Sunday. Sunday is our "heartland" – the place we go to find the power and the guidance we need for the coming week.

4. Spirituality – our relationship with God – needs to go public. Today, churches are often sidelined when critical decisions are made. Its members are not! Our spirituality is often focused on our inner struggles. While we can easily overlook our public lives, that is where we can often do the most for Christ by carrying our Christian values into the world. This is not a matter of imposing our beliefs on others, but rather allowing our faith to guide every facet of our behavior. And that ultimately translates into our ability to influence the individual, social, and political decisions that affect others.

5. A congregation needs to support its members' daily missions. Ideally, this support should be the primary focus of a congregation. When a congregation supports its members in their daily missions, it will discover God's greatest presence and power.

6. We are God's coworkers; Jesus shares his power, the Holy Spirit, with us. When we choose to do God's work, we look to Jesus for help. Jesus overcame evil through his teaching and healing. His resurrection is the ultimate victory over evil. We are not alone when we struggle with evil because Jesus shares with us the Holy Spirit, his power over evil. Evil will never have the final say.

7. Our mission is to live the Gospel. We are here to love each other and to share in God's mission by what we do and say in every part of daily life. We draw on our church's life and worship – our common life and prayer – for the support, guidance, and power to do God's work. The more we see all we do as part of God's mission and the more we believe God is helping us all the time, the more God can help us and the more effective we will be.

SECTION I: HOW TO USE THIS GUIDE

This guide and the activities in it are designed for use by small groups and individuals. Although you can certainly complete most of these activities on your own, you should consider how helpful working with others can be. Others can:

- Help you see things about your daily life that you might not see.
- Help you formulate a plan of action.
- Provide accountability and support.

Consider asking someone in your church for help to find a partner or to form a small study group. Make working alone your last resort, but don't stop if you can't find a partner. If you do decide to work alone, review the leader's guidelines included with each activity for helpful guidance and disregard any instructions that apply to working with partners or in a group.

Supplies

In addition to the activity worksheets included in this guide, you may want to have the following on hand:

- Notebook and pen or pencil.
- Flipchart and markers (to highlight significant ideas in small groups).

Note: We recommend making multiple copies of the activity worksheets in Section IV (pp. 38-51) so that you will always have blank worksheets on hand. Using blank copies makes it easier to determine new missions or to update your worksheets to reflect changes. As you move forward, you will find it very helpful to keep a written record of your work and progress. If you don't want to continue to use the worksheets, do record your new missions in a notebook.

Meeting guidelines for small groups

When working with a small group, it's best to decide together on a place to meet that is convenient for everyone. Your church most likely has a room available for this purpose. At your first group meeting, begin with a prayer for God's help and do the following:

- Ask group members to introduce themselves (if necessary).
- Share contact information.
- Set a time limit for your meetings that is agreeable to all participants.
- Decide on a group leader.
- Discuss how often you want to meet.

The group leader accepts responsibility for making sure the meeting room is available and reminding group members to attend. The leader also helps to guide the discussion and to keep the group on track and focused. You may choose one group leader or decide to share this responsibility with each member taking a turn. We have provided leader's guidelines and instructions within each activity to make this task easier.

At your first meeting, you may also want to work out a schedule for completing the activities. For help, refer to the suggested timeframes included for each activity. Keep in mind that a high quality of work is more important than adhering to a set schedule. Take as much time as you need to pray, work, and reflect on each activity.

Suggestions for group leaders

In addition to the leader's guidelines included with each activity, you may find the following information helpful.

- If possible, find out if you can control the room temperature. People work better if they are not too warm or too cold.
- Some people are more outspoken than others. Encourage participation by asking quieter participants what they think.
- Encourage discussion, but keep the meetings to the time limit agreed to by the group. You can always continue a topic in a subsequent meeting.

We recognize that people have different learning styles. Some participants may be put off by having to write out their answers to the activity questions. To accommodate different learning styles, consider using the following alternative methods for completing the worksheets (p. 23) that are part of Activity 2, which involves the most writing. We recommend that everyone complete the worksheets in this activity for at least two mission fields before deciding that an alternative method will work best for them.

Oral method

Some people are simply more verbal than others and do a better job working out their answers orally. Talking it out and dialogue with others help them to clarify their thinking. The following pattern can be substituted for the eight questions on each worksheet.

- What do you sense God might want you to do in this mission field? [combines questions 1 and 2]

- What, specifically, do you see yourself doing? [combines questions 3, 4, and 5]

- Who might be your teammate and how might you recruit him/her? [question 6]

- When you believe it's time to talk with your teammate about how what you are doing is part of God's mission, how might you do that? [question 7]

- When the time is right – for example, when your teammate gets tired, how will you share how God and the church help you and, so, might help him/her as well? [question 8]

Those who use the oral method often write out their answers later as they come to see the value of a written record of their accomplishments in their faith journey.

Rapid written method

Once people have been through a series of missions, they may find that they know the questions so well that they may want to get right to identifying their next mission. They can run through the questions of the oral method rather quickly and jot down their updates to keep them focused on the next steps. We call this the "rapid written method." Do go through all eight questions in writing for each mission field a number of times before you switch to this rapid written method. Give yourself time to become thoroughly familiar with the process before shortening it.

SECTION II: SIX ACTIVITIES TO DISCOVER AND TO CARRYOUT YOUR DAILY MISSIONS

Leader's guidelines for Section II

The six activities in this section can be done individually or in small groups. Small groups can use these 12 sessions. Groups of five to six participants are optimal for sharing and interaction in 75 to 90 minutes. Such groups meeting weekly might proceed as follows.

Session 1: "The fields of daily life" (Table 1, p. 15); "Activity 1: What am I doing right now to make the world a better place" (pp. 16-17); discuss seeing our activities as missions using "Resource A: Our fields of daily life are our daily mission fields" (p. 56); distribute and discuss "Example A: Jim's and Margaret's missions on a specific day" (pp. 13-14); as their assignment for the next session, distribute the worksheet for Home (p. 39) and the opening of "Activity 2: Discerning my daily missions" (p. 18) through the hints in "Example B: Hints and sample responses for the home and work mission fields" (pp. 19-22 omitting the Leader's guidelines.)

Sessions 2–5: using "Activity 2: Discerning my daily missions" (pp. 18-22), complete and share the worksheets for home, work, community, and wider world (pp. 39-42) in the order named; at the close of each session distribute the next worksheet for completion before the next session.

[Continue or take a break for a few weeks.]

Sessions 6–8: still in "Activity 2: Discerning my daily missions", complete and share the worksheets for leisure, spiritual health, and church life and outreach (as on p. 23); at the end of session 8, distribute the worksheets for "Activity 3: My daily missions at a glance" (p. 46), and "Activity 4: My road map for my daily missions" (p. 47), to complete for the next session and give out the instructions for completing them (pp. 24-27).

Session 9: discuss the completed Activity 3 glance chart (p. 46) and the completed Activity 4 road map (p. 47); each shares his/her progress with one or two of their daily missions.

Session 10: "Activity 5: Discovering God's gifts for my missions" (pp. 28-29).

Session 11: "Activity 6: Finding a teammate" (pp. 30-33); allow 2 hours for this session; pass out Section III (pp. 35-36) to read before Session 12.

Session 12: discuss questions and comments on Section III (pp. 35-36); practice a Bible study method for an ongoing support group (the oral method of *When the Members Are the Missionaries*, pp. 165–167, or on the Web at membermission.org > Vision > Basic Tools > Basic Tools 18).

A way for mutual prayer:

- At the end of each session, each person makes a prayer request about what he/she will do for the coming week.
- Perhaps, ask each person to name the mission field for which his/her prayer request is made
- The requests are listed and given to all for daily use.
- Begin the next session with each sharing specifically, what happened in the area of their request. Expect some "aha" responses when participants recall occasions of God's help they had overlooked.

EXAMPLE A:
Jim's and Margaret's missions on a specific day

We can benefit from hearing about the daily missions of others. The following examples focus on Jim and Margaret, whose work on discerning one of their daily missions appeared in the book, *When the Members Are the Missionaries* (pp. 18–23 and 29–35). We called them a year later and asked them to describe all of their current daily missions. They answered easily. Our intensive work to describe one mission field for the book had taught them how to discern their daily missions in each area of life.

JIM'S MISSIONS THE DAY WE CALLED

Jim and Mary have four young sons. Jim also has a teenage daughter from his first marriage. In the book, he said his home mission was peacekeeping in his blended family. Here are Jim's daily missions on the day of the phone call.

 Home: Jim works at night and takes care of the children during the day so that Mary can work as a teacher and publish her innovations in her field of teaching high school chemistry.

 Work: A dispatcher for a trucking company, he practices preserving harmony and peace by resisting the attempts of coworkers to draw him into excessive contention between labor and management.

 Community: He and Mary work with "Project Graduation," which protects teens by providing an all-night, post-prom party with food, entertainment, and friendly supervision.

 Wider world: He and Mary help with mailings to secure funds for the children's museum in a nearby city.

 Leisure: To reduce the stress of work and child care, he plays golf to relax, recharge, and keep from being short-tempered with his family.

 Spiritual health: He draws on the Lord's Prayer; on Jesus' reminder to love your neighbor as yourself; on the nature of love in 1 Corinthians 13; and on St. Francis' prayer, "Where there is hatred, sow love."

 Church life and outreach: He greets newcomers at coffee hour and church suppers and introduces them to others to help them feel accepted and included.

EXAMPLE A:
Jim's and Margaret's missions on a specific day continued

MARGARET'S MISSIONS THE DAY WE CALLED

Margaret is a single mother with a son in the ninth grade and twin daughters in the sixth grade. In the book, Margaret told about her mission at work to resolve tension with a coworker. Here are Margaret's daily missions on the day of the phone call. See "Example G: A completed glance chart and road map" (pp. 53-55) for examples of Margaret's daily missions on a glance chart and road map.

Home: She talks intentionally and on the appropriate level for each of her children about drugs and alcohol as well as dating boundaries; and about how to cope with life's pressures as Christians.

Work: She offers ideas about how to get new contracts for her office. When her boss asks her opinion, she asks for time to think – often overnight; prays about it; reflects on what to do; and, then, answers. Her boss knows this is her process, and, because her recommendations are sound, he accepts her contemplative procedure.

Community: She works with others to set up a shelter for homeless people in transition. To motivate others to help her, she tells her own story of domestic violence and how the church provided a home for her and her three children so they would not have to sleep in the car.

Wider world: She is concerned about the growing gap between the rich and the poor and is looking for ways to increase opportunities for the poor.

Leisure: She writes about what she calls the "God-shaped vacuum" in each one of us. Her writing will probably lead to an evangelism course for her congregation.

Spiritual health: She participates in a weekly "fourth day" group (an ongoing small group process developed by National Episcopal Cursillo, Conway, South Carolina); continues her own regular Bible reading and study; and listens to Christian music. She is also part of two church groups: one connects daily life and the Bible; the other explores her communion's traditions.

Church life and outreach: She is preparing her son for Confirmation. She and her son and twin daughters are memorizing the Nicene Creed and talking about living the baptismal covenant.

Beginning the discovery

Now you are ready to begin seeing yourself as part of God's mission. This process can seem overwhelming at first; however, you will find that the seven areas of daily life reflect how you actually live. Further, in each of the activities in this section, you will find helpful guidelines, hints, and examples. As you complete each activity, you will see how the work you do for one activity leads into the next and you will find the process becoming easier. Best of all, you will discover a true sense of purpose and empowerment.

To determine what you need to be doing for and with God, you need to look closely at each *field of daily life* as listed in Table 1. For all, hand out this table and the two paragraphs that follow on a separate sheet.

You may be interested to learn that in the 16th century, Martin Luther wrote about four fields of daily life: home, work, community, and church. Today, we also need to consider the wider world beyond our communities. Although you may feel that you work as hard as the medieval serfs of Luther's time, you, at least, get time off. Therefore, we also have added leisure, to our list. We have subdivided the sixth area – the church – into two sections to reflect both your spiritual health and your relationship with the church.

You will complete the activities in this section by considering each of these areas of daily life. These areas are your daily mission fields – which is how we will refer to them throughout the rest of this guide.

Table 1: The fields of daily Life

 Home: includes all in the home and close friends

 Work: includes home management, school, and volunteer work

 Community: neighborhood, town, or city

 The wider world: includes all aspects of the society, culture, economy, government, or environment in the county, state, nation, or world

 Leisure: any activity to rest or refresh yourself

 Spiritual health: your inner life with God and, so, any activity to meet your own spiritual needs.

 Church life and outreach: your part: in your church's life and its outreach in service and evangelism; or in the life of your district, diocese or communion in the U.S. or worldwide church; or in interchurch or interfaith activities.

Note: These areas of daily life are your daily mission fields.

Activity 1: What I am doing right now to make the world a better place

Begin where you are. Right now, you are probably doing things to make the world a more loving and just place. See p. 38 for the worksheet for "Activity 1: What am I doing right now to make the world a better place."

Leader's guidelines

Suggested timeframe: 1 ½ hours

Participants work alone and then share with a partner or two others (allow about 10–15 minutes for individuals to complete the worksheet and 5–7 minutes in pairs or threes to share their activities). If you are working alone, complete the worksheet and use the discussion notes to think about your answers.

After participants have completed the worksheet of Activity 1, follow these discussion notes and invite them to share their thoughts and ideas. As leader, for more background when the group discusses the five marks of a mission, see "Resource A: Our fields of daily life are our daily mission fields" in Section IV (pp. 56-58). Make copies for each participant.

Discussion notes

In the whole group, ask for two activities in each area of daily life – one from a man, one from a woman, if possible.

Next, discuss how these activities are their missions. Mission is the grand name for Christian work. But, how can you know if your daily actions qualify as a mission? A mission has these five characteristics:

- Centers in love and justice.
- Calls for specific actions and words.
- Costs you time and energy.
- Is carried out only with God's help.
- Brings joy.

Be alert to missions that may be self-serving. A self-serving mission:

- Expects something in return.
- Places your personal needs, wants, or schedule over the needs of others.

Do you see how your actions can be called "missions?" How do you feel or think about this name for your daily activities to make the world a better place? Draw on Resource A (pp. 56-58) to work with questions that may arise. Give out copies of Resource A for further study after this discussion.

Recall the missions of Jim and Margaret (Example A, pp. 13-14). You will learn to discern your missions day-by-day as they did.

Keep in mind that missions do change over time. What you believe you are called to do today may change. Old missions end and new ones begin.

Activity 2: Discerning my daily missions

God wants to help you to make life more loving and more just in each area of your daily life right now. That is why, in Activity 2, you will think more deeply about your responses to Activity 1 (p. 16). We have included hints to help you as you consider each question. However, you may have thoughts of your own, so be sure to listen to your inner voice. Before you begin, you may want to pray for God's guidance:

> *Dear Lord, thank you for this time to take a look at my life.*
>
> *I am doing some things I know you want me to do, but I have more work to do.*
>
> *In each area of my life, guide me, give me a vision, and open me to your leading.*
>
> *Thank you for your help and guidance at all times. Amen.*

As you complete Activity 2's worksheets (pp. 39-45), do not feel that you must be led only to newsworthy and exciting missions. God gladly accepts and works with you wherever you are and in whatever you do that is loving and just. Think again about Jesus' story of the harvest (Matthew 20:1–16). Even though some toiled all day in the fields and some worked only an hour, all received the same pay. God values small as well as large works. It's being loving and just in whatever you do that counts. Your work in each mission field opens the possibility for God to make maximum use of your unique combination of talents and abilities. The Lord will put them to good use and help you to shore up any weaknesses.

Leader's guidelines

Adapt the procedure appropriate for your situation:

- Individuals work alone or with a partner at their own pace.
- Small groups – see the outline for sessions 1–12 on pp. 11-12

At single sessions such as a retreat or overview to introduce the member mission vision, distribute and review briefly all of Activity 2 (pp. 18-22) and "Example A: Jim's and Margaret's missions on a specific day" (pp.13-14). Ask participants to select one of the worksheets for a mission field for completion. Allow 5–10 minutes for completion. Then each person shares his/her responses with the others, as guided by "Table 2: Enhancing responses to Activity 2 worksheets" (p. 23). Allow about 7–10 minutes per person for the sharing.

When completing the worksheets for the mission fields (pp. 39-45), it helps to have some hints to guide their completion. For examples of how two people might complete them, distribute and review "Example B: Hints and sample responses for the home and work mission fields" (pp. 19-22).

EXAMPLE B:
Hints and sample responses for the home and work mission fields

A mother finds closeness is lacking in family life. A postal worker copes with an overly demanding manager. These examples show how that mother and postal worker might answer the questions in Activity 2 for the home and work mission fields. As you review these examples, notice that the responses are not what you would think of as being "religious." The mother is not asking the family to begin daily prayer together but speaks naturally about God's help and opens the door for them to participate in activities that will increase closeness. The postal worker knows that most of his coworkers are not churchgoers so he is careful to talk about God indirectly.

Note also that seeking a teammate is part of your mission. Follow Jesus' wisdom in sending out disciples in pairs (Mark 6:7). While time or circumstances may make finding a teammate neither practical nor possible, questions 6, 7, and 8 will prepare you to seek a helper should the unfolding of your mission call for it.

1. What has God been doing in (this mission field)? What message am I getting about it? Try a response beginning with: I believe God is . . .

Hint: Be guided by where you see love and justice at work or where they are needed or are weak. Here are some places to look for clues for what God is doing or saying. If you've made mistakes in the past, remember God forgives; try to figure out the Lord's current message for you and get ready to try again. Or, what's foremost in your mind in this area? What really needs to be fixed or changed? What are others saying to you that sticks in your mind? What is happening around you? What do you sense that you want to do or should be doing? Do you sense a need to confront and seek to correct some wrongdoing or evil in this area of life? Do you see anything blocking love or justice? Or any way in which love and justice need to be increased? Cite God; avoid a wholly secular answer.

 Home example: *a mother senses this message:* I believe that God is telling me that our family life is fractured. We are not as close as we could be.

 Work example: *a worker senses this message:* I believe God is telling me to speak up about the unfair workload that all of us share.

2. As I think about God's message, what is my vision or goal for how I want life to be in (this mission field)?

Hint: A vision is a general statement and provides you with a sense of direction, such as "My vision is to have a close working relationship with my team at work." A goal is a concrete step that is clear and specific; for example, "My goal is to meet with my manager regularly for better communication." Word your vision or goal to be direct and expressed in a simple sentence.

 Home example: My vision is for my family to spend more time together and enjoy it free of outside distractions.

 Work example: My goal is to start speaking up about unfair treatment.

EXAMPLE B:
Hints and sample responses for the home and work mission fields continued

3 **What am I doing right now to make this vision or goal a reality?**

Hint: Name even the smallest effort. Do be honest if you're not doing anything to work toward making your vision or goal a reality. Say so here and let the hints for the next question stimulate your imagination.

Home example: I am trying to get us to find a regular family time to talk, laugh, and share what we are doing outside the family.

Work example: I am trying to get to know my coworkers better and to find common ground with each of them.

4 **What do I still need to do? Begin with thinking of where you need to bring or to increase caring or love, fairness or justice; and working with your gifts, limitations, and convictions.**

Hint: Once you get a feeling or idea as to what you might do, write it down – even if you don't think you have it quite right. Guard against the fear of failure that can sometimes inhibit concrete goal setting. Lean on God's unlimited help. Perhaps you will try again to do something that you did not do well in the past.

Home example: I need to turn off all the distractions in the evening and work on getting my family to set aside some time to pay attention to one another.

Work example: I want to be able to speak up when the manager is being unfair.

5 **What, specifically, will I do or continue to do to make my vision or goal a reality and when will I do it? Limit yourself to just one action. This is or will be your mission in (this mission field).**

Hint: So far, you have answered thinking and planning questions. The remaining questions are action-oriented and require concrete answers. Answer question 5 by writing down the *specific action* you will take and *when* you will take it.

Home example: I'll work toward spending every Tuesday night eating together and doing something as a family with no distractions. If we can just do this three times starting next Tuesday, I'll feel we've gotten started and I'll look forward to going on from there.

Work example: I need to speak up the very next time we're not being treated fairly.

Living the Gospel: A Guide for Individuals and Small Groups

EXAMPLE B:
Hints and sample responses for the home and work mission fields continued

6 **Who can work with me to carry out this mission? How will I describe the mission to interest him/her? Answer with the person's name and words you might actually use.**

Hint: A mission works better with a teammate who knows what you are trying to do (Mark 6:7), who regularly checks on your progress, and who offers whatever insight he or she has. Such a teammate will help you to achieve needed and lasting change. Also, think broadly. Who is most able to help you? Don't exclude potential teammates who may not be religious. Choose anyone who is committed to love and justice as primary values. They already share in God's mission of love and justice even though they do not know it. Further, put your mission in appealing words to help your desired teammate to say "yes." Does your invitation sound inviting? Note: you may want to recruit more than one teammate as you see the postal worker recruiting Tom and Hank (below). We have kept all the references to finding a teammate in the singular for simplicity. Recruit as many as you believe you need. Use the same procedures for each one.

 Home example: I'll need my husband to agree to help me to get things going. I could say something like, "I bet you want more family time as much as I do. Let's do a family night once a week – no computers, TV, or video games. Let's just take time to do something together. What do you think? Will you help me get this started?"

Work example: "Tom and Hank, can I check with you when I have something to bring up to make sure that what I have in mind is something that's important to all of us? If you keep me on track, I believe we can make a difference."

7 **When the time is right, how can I explain how what we are doing is or can be part of God's mission? Answer with words you might actually use.**

Hint: Words, as well as actions, make up a full mission. Mention how this work connects with God, God's mission, your faith, the Bible, or the church. Be yourself and use everyday words. Think also about the best time to talk this way with your teammate such as when the mission becomes quite difficult. Do ask for permission.

 Home example: I might say, "Can I share what I believe about this?…Since I've been going to church these last few months, I've been thinking about how I'd really like for our family to be closer. The kids are growing up so fast I feel I hardly know them."

Work example: "Can I share what I believe about this?…I believe we are made to work together so that everyone feels that they matter and are heard."

8 **When the time is right, how could I encourage my teammate to turn to the church for help and support? Begin with how church helps you; that may give you an idea of what to suggest for how it might help him or her. Answer with words you might actually use.**

Hint: Thinking of how your church actually helps you in this mission field might give you an idea as to how it might help him/her. You are not burdening your teammate. He/she needs to know where you go for help so that he/she might find help there too. If not a churchgoer, hearing how the church helps you can open the door to a dimension

EXAMPLE B:
Hints and sample responses for the home and work mission fields continued

of church life that may be new to him/her. If a churchgoer, your sharing is a useful affirming of the power available to us in church life. Do ask for permission to share before you begin. [If you, yourself, are not a churchgoer, you may find yourself inclined to seek out a church as you take up your daily missions. When you sense that prayer and church life are giving you some needed power for daily life, share that with your teammate. You may even suggest you can pray together. Remember that you can always come back to this question later.]

 Home example: My husband is a Christmas and Easter worshiper, so I might say, "Can I share what helps me that might help you too?…Come to church with me for a few Sundays. My week always seems to go better when I've been to church. See if that happens for you, too. Maybe, while we're there – or another time – we can pray for our family time to go well."

 Work example: Most of my coworkers are not churchgoers, so I don't push. I'll talk about God indirectly. If I speak up and it makes a difference, I'll be ready to say something like, "Can I tell you what I am thinking?…I think we made some progress. We must be getting help from somewhere." They may change the subject but I will usually hear something later that tells me they heard me suggesting that help came from beyond us and that they might ask for such help themselves.

Notes for sharing worksheets

To ensure effective sharing of these daily mission worksheets, follow these steps.

1. Review "Table 2: Enhancing responses to Activity 2 worksheets" (below); also print and distribute Table 2 and the paragraph that follows it for use by everyone.

2. Work with a partner or group of three to five to share responses.

3. After each person shares, the other participants, guided by Table 2, affirm the sharing and, where needed, suggest what might enhance it.

4. If the person sharing has difficulty answering a question (such as 7 and 8), the rest try to "be that person" and to come up with an answer.

Table 2: Enhancing responses to Activity 2 worksheets	
Question 1	Is this response *clear*? Is God *mentioned*? Clarity is more important than theological accuracy. Avoid a wholly secular answer.
Questions 2, 3, and 4	Did you get the sense that the responses to these questions are *leading up to question 5*?
Question 5	This is the key question. Does it state a *specific action* and *when* it will be done? Can you tell what the person is going to do and when?
Question 6	Does the response name a *specific person*? Does the description of the mission sound *inviting*?
Question 7	Is the explanation *clear*? Make explicit reference to God, God's mission, your faith, the Bible, or the church.
Question 8	Is the description of how the church helps the member and how it might help the other phrased in *clear and specific terms*?

Note and discuss how essential questions 7 and 8 are to the fullness of mission. A mission always has two parts – what we do and what we say about God. The word without the deed is empty; the deed without the word is dark. Still further, if your teammate is not a church member, a mission is incomplete until we have invited him/her to join Jesus' people and his mission. As noted in the hints above, if your teammate is not a churchgoer, hearing how the church helps you can open the door to a dimension of church life that may be new to him or to her. If what you share is already familiar to your teammate, your sharing is still a useful affirming of the power available to us in church life. Questions 7 and 8 are much of what we know as evangelism. This member mission process puts evangelism inside of mission where it should have been all along. This sharing will take less time than telling your story and will, probably, be heard much more deeply.

Activity 3: My daily missions at a glance

At this point, you have completed a huge amount of work. You have discerned your present mission for each of your mission fields. Now you need a way to condense your ideas so that you can move ahead more easily. In this activity, you will condense your answers from the Activity 2 worksheets (pp. 39-45) into a word or phrase that expresses the main idea(s) on a chart. This activity will give you a snapshot of your daily missions. It can be done at home and brought to the next session, or it can be done as a group. In a group, allow 25 to 35 minutes for participants as they work alone – about three to four minutes per mission field.

Leader's guidelines

If this activity is done at home, review the following at the end of sharing the church mission field worksheets. If the activity is done as a group, ask participants to

- Review "Example C: My daily missions at a glance – two sample columns" (p. 25).

- For a sample of a completed glance chart, see pp. 53-54. Margaret is the working mother whose mission at work is reported in *When the Members Are the Missionaries*, pp. 29–35. This chart lists all of her missions on the particular day we talked by phone a year later.

- Complete the "Activity 3: Worksheet – My daily missions at a glance" (see p. 46) for each mission field using just a key word or short phrase to condense the main ideas. Fill in all the boxes, even the shaded ones, and note that they will use the information in the shaded boxes in Activity 4.

- Discuss their feelings, comments, and what they have learned from this activity.

EXAMPLE C:
My daily missions at a glance – two sample columns

	HOME (mother)	WORK (postal worker)
1. What has God been doing in this mission field? What message am I getting?	my family life is fractured	speak up about the unfair workload
2. As I think about God's message, what is my vision or goal for this mission field?	spend more time together and enjoy it	start speaking up about unfair treatment
3. What am I doing right now to make this vision or goal a reality?	trying to get time together to talk about the day	know my coworkers better and find common ground
4. What do I still need to do?	turn off all distractions so we can focus on one another	be able to speak up when the boss is unfair
5. What, specifically, will I do to make my vision or goal a reality? When will I do it?	have a family night on Tuesday for three weeks	speak up the next time we are treated unfairly
6. Who can work with me to carry out this mission? How will I interest him/her?	my husband: "I bet you want more family time as much as I do"	Tom and Hank: "We can make a difference"
7. How will I talk about being part of God's mission with my teammate?	"church has led me to want a closer family"	"I believe we are made to work together"
8. How will I encourage my teammate to turn to the church for help and support?	"my week goes better – might happen for you"	"we made progress – we must be getting help from somewhere"

Activity 4: My road map for my daily missions

You will find your road map of your daily missions to be a living document designed to help you build a new and better life step by step – one that is more purposeful and directed. Fitting the missions on your road map into your busy days can be challenging. But, what matters more in your day – getting the car's oil changed or spending time with your troubled family member, friend, or loved one? You won't always remember whether you changed the oil on time, but you will surely remember not spending enough time with your loved one. In fact, that may well be all you remember. If you complete nothing else, but have moved one step closer to achieving one of your missions, then your day was a success! So review your road map with its daily missions often and pray for the power, wisdom, and guidance to focus on and to carry them out.

In this activity, you will take your responses to Activity 3 (your completed glance chart from p. 46) and condense them further to get a clear picture of your

- Vision/goal (Question 2 on the glance chart).
- Teammate (Question 6 on the glance chart).
- Mission (Question 5 on the glance chart).

This activity can be done at home and brought to the next session along with the glance chart (p. 46) or it can be done as a group. Whether working alone or in a group, allow 15 to 25 minutes.

Leader's guidelines

Print, hand out, and review this page with "Example D: Sample road map for my home and work mission fields" (p. 27).

Ask participants to:

- View Margaret's completed road map on pp. 53-55.
- Transfer their comments from the shaded areas on the glance chart to the blank spaces on the "Activity 4: Worksheet – My road map for my daily missions" (p. 47).
- Be sure to record a date to start working on each mission in the mission column of the worksheet.
- Discuss their feelings, comments, and what they have learned from this activity.
- Keep their completed road maps handy to stay on track and remain focused. Put them on the refrigerator door or on a mirror used daily.

EXAMPLE D:
Sample road map for my home and work mission fields

	VISION/GOAL (question 2 from Activity 3)	TEAMMATE (question 6 from Activity 3 – how to interest to him or her)	MISSION (question 5 from Activity 3 – what to do or action/s to take and when to start)
HOME	spend more time together and enjoy it	my husband: "I bet you want more family time as much as I do"	have a family night on Tuesday for three weeks, start next Tuesday
WORK	start speaking up about unfair treatment	Tom and Hank: "we can make a difference"	speak up the next time we are treated unfairly
COMMUNITY			
WIDER WORLD			
LEISURE			
SPIRITUAL HEALTH			
CHURCH LIFE AND OUTREACH			

Section II 27

Activity 5: Discovering God's gifts for my missions

On completing your road map, you might feel a range of emotions from relief and joy to concern about the significant amount of work you still have to do and the struggle involved. Take heart. All of us struggle with evil which blocks love and justice. By drawing on God's gifts, we can cast out the demons of hard hearts, cruel people, poor governments, or exploitative corporations. God, Jesus, the Holy Spirit, the church, the sacraments, the Bible – these are our anchors and places of safety and love, guidance and power. Jesus sends us on mission as he sent the twelve disciples. You, too, are given or will be given the gifts you need to carry out your missions. Recall again John 20:21–22.

In Activity 5, you will identify the gifts you already have and the gifts you will need to carry out your missions. Do not be limited to the gifts listed by Paul in Romans 12:6–8, 1 Corinthians 12:8–10, and Ephesians 4:11–12, such as the gifts of prophecy or discernment of spirits. Those lists were his words for gifts for church life of the first century. Make your own lists for this century and see gifts in all the areas of daily life, not just in church life (see Table 3, p. 29, and distribute a copy for each group member).

You should not feel concerned if you think you lack the gifts needed to accomplish your missions. If God gave you the mission, then God will also give you the gifts – or a partner who has them – to complete it. You may even discover gifts you did not know you had simply because you hadn't used them until a specific mission brought them into play.

Leader's guidelines

Suggested timeframe: allow 10 to 15 minutes per person

We recommend completing Activity 5 in groups of two or three. Another's perspective can help you to clarify the gifts you already have or the gifts you will need to carry out your mission. If you are working on your own, you might share your thoughts with a friend or relative.

Ask participants to:

- Review "Table 3: God's gifts to us" (p. 29).
- Form groups of two or three.
- Each selects his or her most important daily mission.
- Each describes the selected daily mission in detail to the group.

As each person finishes sharing, the others cite the gifts they perceive at work or may still be required. List them on a flip chart. The sharer responds with comments or questions. Then, the group prays for the sharer. Following is a suggested prayer.

Dear Lord, please increase the gifts you have given _____.

Please provide the gifts or help that _____ needs to carry out (his/her) mission

Thank you, Lord, for the help and love you provide every day.

When all have finished sharing, have the group discuss their feelings, what they have learned, or questions they may have regarding gifts for their daily missions. Suggest that participants write in the gifts they need on their road maps.

Table 3: God's gifts to us	
GIFT	**EXAMPLES**
Advocacy	Defending those who cannot defend themselves. *Example: Helping poor children to get health coverage.*
Coaching	Helping others develop valuable skills. *Example: Working with a girls' or boys' soccer team.*
Communication	Turning thoughts into words that others can understand; and putting them in a way that encourages further discussion. *Example: Discussing issues of the day without having to win.*
Imagination	Seeing new possibilities *Example: A unique idea to help underachieving youth.*
Intuition	Sensing the needs of others. *Example: Recognizing when a friend needs to talk or needs someone to listen.*
Monitoring	Keeping track of systems or events. *Example: Helpful oversight of others focused on enabling their success, not on criticizing them.*
Organization	Pulling together different parts into a cohesive whole. *Example: Coordinating the work of an auto repair shop.*
Self Knowledge	Understanding your talents and limitations. *Example: Knowing how much energy you can devote to helping others.*
Hospitality	Helping others to feel at ease. *Example: Helping church visitors to meet others at coffee hour.*

Activity 6: Finding a teammate

Often, God's work is best done as a team. Jesus called people to join him in his mission (see Mark 1:17, 2:14, and 3:13-15) and he sent them out to do his work in pairs (see Mark 6:7). You need teammates to achieve needed and lasting change. When you seek a teammate, you participate in evangelism. The term "evangelism" might bring to mind that pamphlet-bearing person who comes to your door and starts preaching whether or not you are prepared to listen. You are not involved in that kind of evangelism! Rather, in your actions for love and justice, you provide a context for your words that speaks louder than any pamphlet ever could.

Further, drawing nonchurch people into your missions of love and justice draws them into Jesus' mission. Although they may not see themselves as Jesus' agents, you do. You look ahead to a time when you can talk explicitly about your work as part of God's mission and the possibility of their conscious commitment to it. As for church people, drawing them into your mission refreshes their own commitment to Jesus and his mission. You do both with the Holy Spirit's help. You are being a true New Testament evangelist.

As in the worksheets of Activity 2 (pp. 39-45), you prepare to talk about God and the church here as well. You might worry that your teammate does not want to hear about God and the church. Just remember that your talk about God and the church helps your teammate to know you better. Your teammate has a right to know the basis of your actions and where you find the power to do them. This is not an intrusion into someone else's life, but a sharing of who you are. It may be the most powerful "storytelling" you ever do. You are not saying, "I want you to believe as I do." You are saying, "This is how God is real for me and – who knows God might become real for you, too." In this activity, you are a life-centered and mission-centered evangelist.

This practice of finding a teammate can be a rich learning experience. You will be better prepared and more at ease when you actually seek a teammate after this activity. In this activity, you will practice finding a teammate by doing some role playing.

Leader's guidelines

Suggested timeframe: 2 hours

Participants work in groups of three. (Allow about 10 minutes for participants to complete the worksheet and about 45–60 minutes for each trio to complete the role-play practice, and 10-15 minutes to reflect on the role play.) If you are working on your own, review the exercise and try practicing with a friend or relative.

Ask participants to do the following:
- Each chooses the mission from the worksheets of Activity 2 for which he or she wants a teammate the most.

- Distribute and review "Example E: Finding a teammate at work" (p.32) with "Activity 6: Worksheets – Finding a teammate" (pp. 48-51) in hand. Note how the stories in Example E match the questions of the Activity 6 worksheets.

- For actual stories, review "Example F: Finding a teammate – Stories" (p.33).

- Complete the Activity 6 worksheets. Keep these worksheets in hand or nearby for reference as needed during the role play.

- Break up into groups of three for the role play and move to separate areas so that the groups can work simultaneously without bothering each other.

- Because leading successful role playing is a subtle process, see and follow "Resource B: Four steps to practice finding a teammate" (pp. 58-59). Distribute copies to each participant.

Discussion notes: Point out that participants should always be ready to go through all the steps in finding a teammate, but sometimes it's better to wait for an appropriate time for Steps 7 and 8 in the process. The guiding principle is to meet people where they are and to involve them in what we believe to be God's work.

- See that all the trios complete three rounds of the role play and reflect on their learnings for 10-15 minutes.

- Reassemble the whole group. Allow 10-15 minutes for this plenary session.

- Ask them to share some of their learnings.

- Clarify any confusion that arises; answer questions.

To close: Ask participants to read "Section III: Making Decisions and Moving Ahead." (pp. 35-36). Be prepared to discuss the decision-making process outlined in that section, to answer questions, and to share ideas about it at the start of the next session as in Session 12 (p. 12).

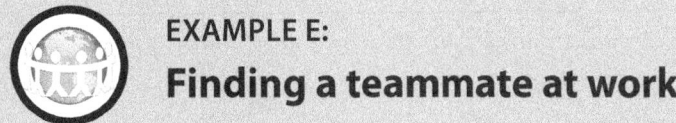

EXAMPLE E:
Finding a teammate at work

Read this example with the Activity 6 worksheets (pp. 48-51) in hand. Notice how Pete's actions relate to the steps for finding a teammate shown on the Activity 6 worksheets.

Pete works for a manager who routinely steals ideas from his staff. As a result, employee morale is at a new low; several workers have left; and others are considering leaving. For his work mission, Pete wants to change the workplace so that all employees are valued and honored for their contributions **(Step 1)**. He knows Rachel and Ben share his concern and thinks they will make good teammates. He knows that Ben is a church member but has no idea about Rachel's religious convictions **(Step 2)**. Pete thinks out ways to describe his vision that might appeal to either of them; and, if the response is positive, how he might ask for help **(Step 3)**. For example, he might say, "Our boss is not a bad person. I can see him being willing to share the spotlight. He just needs some help. Would you help me figure out what to do?"

As a Christian, Pete knows that God cares about all aspects of our lives, but realizes others may not know this. He relies on the love and justice involved in his mission to provide the basis for talking about God and he knows it's important to be brief and to the point **(Step 4)**. Here are examples of what, with permission, he might say:

To a religious person: "I believe God wants our ideas to be valued and respected. We should be recognized for what we contribute."

To a nonreligious person: "My faith means a lot to me. I believe God, also, wants things to be better and for us to be given credit for our ideas."

Pete knows that he must choose a time that feels right to describe how church life and worship help him and might, also, help Rachel or Ben **(Step 5)**. With God's help, his knowledge of his coworkers will help him find the appropriate time and way. Then, he might say, "You know, church restores my hope for a better world and helps me to keep at it. God is at work out there in the world and never gives up. And worshiping in church with others who are trying to live the same way helps me know I am not alone. It might help you, too."

At this point, Pete is ready to go to the potential teammate, share the vision, and ask for help **(Step 6)**. As Pete works with his teammates he can, when he finds the time is right, talk about God's connection to his vision as he sees it **(Step 7)**. When the time is right, such as when the teammate expresses weariness with the mission, Pete is ready to share how church life and worship help him, to share how the teammate might find similar help there, and to offer to help the teammate to explore that possibility **(Step 8)**. Pete trusts that the more deeply they share in the church's message – the Gospel (p. 4) – the more effective they will be. He has found that the more he turns to God for help, the more God can help him.

EXAMPLE F:
Finding a teammate – stories

As you read these actual stories, you will find some of the eight steps present; where they are not present, you will find them either implied or needed later.

Susan: Susan, a representative on the city council, wanted to revive a large, rundown park by starting a farmer's market there. She believed the park commissioner would make a good teammate and asked him, "Can you imagine what the park might become again?" Then, she shared her vision: the park would become a focal point for the community and might one day include a senior center, a swimming pool, a YMCA/YWCA, tennis courts, and a sports stadium. When she asked for his help, the commissioner agreed to work with her. For Susan, starting the farmer's market was an acknowledgment that God made us to live together in community and to provide each other with safe and pleasant places to live. Susan did not talk much about God or church to the commissioner because she thought it was not the right time, but she will do so should the opportunity arise. In the meantime, she has the teammate she needs to help her to realize her vision.

Jim: You may recall Jim from Example A (p. 13) who was working nights and taking care of the children during the day while his wife Mary worked as a teacher. He was getting irritable at home because he never got a break. He shared his concerns with Mary and wondered if playing golf would give him the break he needed. For Jim, requesting something for himself was a big breakthrough. Mary valued Jim's mission for peacemaking at home and understood that leisure time would help to support it. To gain his wife's help, Jim needed only to tell her about the help he needed for this mission at home. She agreed to plan four to five hours twice a month for him to play and sealed the promise with a gift of new clubs.

Phil: Phil is deeply committed to politics. His vision is for every voice to be heard and he works to get voters out on election day. Dee and Jill had expressed readiness to be involved in some way. When Phil met with them, he said, "I hope you don't mind my sharing a bit about myself here. I believe God wants everyone to vote and I want to help to make that happen." Phil did not mention going to church but will later when the time is right. Dee and Jill were not put off by his carefully chosen words and, when asked for their help, both agreed to work with him on this mission in the wider world.

Amy: [While unusual, this is a true story.] Amy's teen son had fallen in with a group that used drugs, and his grades were dropping. Amy knew her son liked to help people – he loved to help with church dinners – and to make new friends. She mentioned her concerns to a church friend and said, "I wish I knew another mom with the same concerns!" Her friend said, "My neighbor Endice is in the same situation. Let me get the two of you together." Amy gasped, saying, "I never heard that name before until two nights ago. I had a dream that ended with someone telling me to help Endice!"

SECTION III: MAKING DECISIONS AND MOVING AHEAD

We all have to make decisions – large and small – every day and some of them can be very difficult. You will make a lot of decisions as you discern your daily missions; as you plan to carry them out; and as you seek teammates to help you. What can help you to discern God's will for your daily missions and the specific decisions needed to work them out? Humanity has wrestled with these questions in every generation! We have provided some decision-making factors to guide your decision-making processes (see Table 4 below). After considering these factors, make your decision, and ask God to help you to carry it out where it is right and to help you to make any needed corrections where it is wrong.

Table 4: A guide for Christian decision making	
Decision-making factors	**Description**
Alternatives	Outline and weigh other possible choices.
Motives	Examine your motives and base your choice on love and justice. Try to be honest about self-serving, hidden, or unconscious motives.
Ends	Check that your goal is based on love and justice.
Means	Think about how you will go about achieving your goals. Restrain any self-interest and work for the greater good for everyone involved.
Outcomes	Anticipate the possible outcomes. Determine which one will be better for all involved – or at least as many others as possible.
Note: For more information on decision making, read *When the Members Are the Missionaries*, Chapter 11, "Decision Making for Missionaries," pp. 129–132.	

In Sections I, II and III, you have worked in depth to discover how to live out your missions in each area of daily life. You have been in dialog with the Lord throughout the process and the Lord will walk with you every step of the way. Discerning your daily missions can be the best spiritual formation of all.

Remember, your contributions cannot be duplicated by anyone else. Your missions are as unique as you are. As you start to work on your missions, you will find your life filled with joy and satisfaction. You will see yourself sharing in God's work and you will feel right – right down to your bones. Start today. Make our world a better place in the ways that, with God's continuing help, only you can.

As you move forward, try to offer every day to God and pray for help and guidance to carry out your daily missions. In each field of life, be ready to make new plans as you complete each mission.

May God bless you with peace and power!

SECTION IV: WORKSHEETS, EXAMPLES, TABLES, AND RESOURCES

ACTIVITY 1: WORKSHEET:
What I am doing right now to make the world a better place

Instructions: Jot down what you're doing in each of the following areas to make life better, more loving and more just. Write down big things such as what you do as a volunteer in a hospital, or as an elected public officer, or as a courteous clerk. Name also even the smallest thing such as always giving up your seat on the bus to an elderly person or being the one in your office who circulates birthday cards for others to sign. The key for a small mission is for the activity to be habitual or usual. It's what you try to do all of the time.

1. Home (includes all in the home and close friends):

2. Work (includes home management, school, and volunteer work):

3. Community (your neighborhood, town, or city):

4. Wider world (includes all aspects of the society, culture, economy, government, or environment of the county, state, nation, or world):

5. Leisure (any activity to rest and to refresh yourself):

6. Church – in two distinct but related aspects (*if you are not now a church member, you may want to skip one or both parts*):

a. My own spiritual health (your inner life with God and, so, any activity to meet your own spiritual needs):

b. My part in our church's life and outreach in service and evangelism (in the congregation, district, diocese, or communion in the U.S. or worldwide church; or in interchurch or interfaith activities):

ACTIVITY 2: WORKSHEET 1 for discerning my daily missions:

Home
(a current mission or one I will begin)

1. What has God been doing in my home life (includes all in the home and close friends)? What message am I getting about it? Try beginning with: I believe God is . . .

2. As I think about God's message, what is my vision or goal for how I want life to be at home?

3. What am I doing right now to make this vision or goal a reality?

4. What do I still need to do? Begin with thinking of where you need to bring or to increase caring or love, fairness or justice; and working with your gifts, limitations, and convictions.

5. What specifically will I do or continue to do to make my vision or goal a reality and when will I do it? Limit yourself to just one action. This is or will be your mission in your home.

6. Who can work with me to carry out this mission? How will I describe the mission to interest him or her? Answer with the person's name and words you might actually use.

7. When the time is right and with permission, how can I explain how what we are doing is or can be part of God's mission? Answer with words you might actually use.

8. When the time is right and with permission, how could I encourage my teammate to turn to the church for help and support? Begin with how the church helps you; that may give you an idea of what to suggest for how it might help him or her. Answer with words you might actually use.

ACTIVITY 2: WORKSHEET 2 for discerning my daily missions:

Work
(a current mission or one I will begin)

1. What has God been doing in my work life (includes home management, school, and volunteer work)? What message am I getting about it? Try beginning with: I believe God is . . .

2. As I think about God's message, what is my vision or goal for how I want life to be at work?

3. What am I doing right now to make this vision or goal a reality?

4. What do I still need to do? Begin with thinking of where you need to bring or to increase caring or love, fairness or justice; and working with your gifts, limitations, and convictions.

5. What specifically will I do or continue to do to make my vision or goal a reality and when will I do it? Limit yourself to just one action. This is or will be your mission in your work.

6. Who can work with me to carry out this mission? How will I describe the mission to interest him or her? Answer with the person's name and words you might actually use.

7. When the time is right and with permission, how can I explain how what we are doing is or can be part of God's mission? Answer with words you might actually use.

8. When the time is right and with permission, how could I encourage my teammate to turn to the church for help and support? Begin with how the church helps you; that may give you an idea of what to suggest for how it might help him or her. Answer with words you might actually use.

ACTIVITY 2: WORKSHEET 3 for discerning my daily missions:

Community
(a current mission or one I will begin)

1. What has God been doing in my community (my neighborhood, town, or city)? What message am I getting about it? Try beginning with: I believe God is . . .

2. As I think about God's message, what is my vision or goal for how I want life to be in my community?

3. What am I doing right now to make this vision or goal a reality?

4. What do I still need to do? Begin with thinking of where you need to bring or to increase caring or love, fairness or justice; and working with your gifts, limitations, and convictions.

5. What specifically will I do or continue to do to make my vision or goal a reality and when will I do it? Limit yourself to just one action. This is or will be your mission in your community.

6. Who can work with me to carry out this mission? How will I describe the mission to interest him or her? Answer with the person's name and words you might actually use.

7. When the time is right and with permission, how can I explain how what we are doing is or can be part of God's mission? Answer with words you might actually use.

8. When the time is right and with permission, how could I encourage my teammate to turn to the church for help and support? Begin with how the church helps you; that may give you an idea of what to suggest for how it might help him or her. Answer with words you might actually use.

ACTIVITY 2: WORKSHEET 4 for discerning my daily missions:

Wider world
(a current mission or one I will begin)

1. What has God been doing in the society, culture, economy, government, or environment of the county, state, nation, or world? What message am I getting? Try beginning with: I believe God is . . .

2. As I think about God's message, what is my vision or goal for how I want life to be in the wider world?

3. What am I doing right now to make this vision or goal a reality?

4. What do I still need to do? Begin with thinking of where you need to bring or to increase caring or love, fairness or justice; and working with your gifts, limitations, and convictions.

5. What, specifically, will I do or continue to do to make my vision or goal a reality and when will I do it? Limit yourself to just one action. This is or will be your mission in the wider world.

6. Who can work with me to carry out this mission? How will I describe the mission to interest him or her? Answer with the person's name and words you might actually use.

7. When the time is right and with permission, how can I explain how what we are doing is or can be part of God's mission? Answer with words you might actually use.

8. When the time is right and with permission, how could I encourage my teammate to turn to the church for help and support? Begin with how the church helps you; that may give you an idea of what to suggest for how it might help him or her. Answer with words you might actually use.

ACTIVITY 2: WORKSHEET 5 for discerning my daily missions:

Leisure
(a current mission or one I will begin)

1. What has God been doing in or telling me about my leisure time (includes any activity that rests or refreshes me)? What message am I getting about it? Try beginning with: I believe God is . . .

2. As I think about God's message, what is my vision or goal for how I want life to be in my leisure time?

3. What am I doing right now to make this vision or goal a reality?

4. What do I still need to do? Begin with thinking of where you need to bring or to increase caring or love, fairness or justice; and working with your gifts, limitations, and convictions.

5. What specifically will I do or continue to do to make my vision or goal a reality and when will I do it? Limit yourself to just one action. This is or will be your mission in your leisure.

6. Who can work with me to carry out this mission? How will I describe the mission to interest him or her? Answer with the person's name and words you might actually use.

7. When the time is right and with permission, how can I explain how what we are doing is or can be part of God's mission? Answer with words you might actually use.

8. When the time is right and with permission, how could I encourage my teammate to turn to the church for help and support? Begin with how the church helps you; that may give you an idea of what to suggest for how it might help him or her. Answer with words you might actually use.

ACTIVITY 2: WORKSHEET 6 for discerning my daily missions:

Spiritual health
(a current mission or one I will begin)

1 What has God been doing in or telling me about my own spiritual health (my inner life with God and, so, any activity to meet my own spiritual needs)? What message am I getting about it? Try beginning with: I believe God is . . .

2 As I think about God's message, what is my vision or goal for what I want for my spiritual health?

3 What am I doing right now to make this vision or goal a reality?

4 What do I still need to do? Begin with thinking of where you need to bring or to increase caring or love, fairness or justice; and working with your gifts, limitations, and convictions.

5 What specifically will I do or continue to do to make my vision or goal a reality and when will I do it? Limit yourself to just one action. This is or will be your mission for your spiritual health.

6 Who can work with me to carry out this mission? How will I describe the mission to interest him or her? Answer with the person's name and words you might actually use.

7 When the time is right and with permission, how can I explain how what we are doing is or can be part of God's mission? Answer with words you might actually use.

8 When the time is right and with permission, how could I encourage my teammate to turn to the church for help and support? Begin with how the church helps you; that may give you an idea of what to suggest for how it might help him or her. Answer with words you might actually use.

ACTIVITY 2: WORKSHEET 7 for discerning my daily missions:
Church life and outreach
(a current mission or one I will begin)

1. What has God been doing in my part: in my church's life and its outreach in service and evangelism; or in the life of my district, diocese, or communion in the U.S. or worldwide church; or in interchurch or interfaith activities? What message am I getting about it? Try beginning with: I believe God is . . .

2. As I think about God's message, what is my vision or goal for how I want to participate in my church's life and outreach?

3. What am I doing right now to make this vision or goal a reality?

4. What do I still need to do? Begin with thinking of where you need to bring or to increase caring or love, fairness or justice; and working with your gifts, limitations, and convictions.

5. What specifically will I do or continue to do to make my vision or goal a reality and when will I do it? Limit yourself to just one action. This is or will be your mission in your church's life and outreach.

6. Who can work with me to carry out this mission? How will I describe the mission to interest him or her? Answer with the person's name and words you might actually use.

7. When the time is right and with permission, how can I explain how what we are doing is or can be part of God's mission? Answer with words you might actually use.

8. When the time is right and with permission, how could I encourage my teammate to turn to the church for help and support? Begin with how the church helps you; that may give you an idea of what to suggest for how it might help him or her. Answer with words you might actually use.

ACTIVITY 3: WORKSHEET:
My daily missions at a glance

	HOME	WORK	COMMUNITY	WIDER WORLD	LEISURE	SPIRITUAL HEALTH	CHURCH LIFE AND OUTREACH
1. What has God been doing in this mission field? What message am I getting?							
2. As I think about God's message, what is my vision or goal for this mission field?							
3. What am I doing right now to make this vision or goal a reality?							
4. What do I still need to do?							
5. What, specifically, will I do to make my vision or goal a reality? When will I do it?							
6. Who can work with me to carry out this mission? How will I interest him or her?							
7. How can I talk about being part of God's mission with my teammate?							
8. How could I encourage my teammate to turn to the church for help and support?							

ACTIVITY 4: WORKSHEET:
My road map for my daily missions

	VISION/GOAL (question 2 from Activity 3)	**TEAMMATE** (question 6 from Activity 3 – how to interest him or her)	**MISSION** (question 5 from Activity 3 – what to do or action/s to take and when to start)
HOME			
WORK			
COMMUNITY			
WIDER WORLD			
LEISURE			
SPIRITUAL HEALTH			
CHURCH LIFE AND OUTREACH			

ACTIVITY 6: WORKSHEETS:
Finding a teammate

Note: Steps 1 through 5 are your preparation for finding a teammate. Steps 6 through 8 are the actions you take. Note the variations from step 3 (p. 50) on that are suited for a potential teammate who is not religious. Select the mission you want help with the most and have in hand the worksheet from Activity 2 for that mission field. See hints below and "Example E: Finding a teammate at work" (p. 32) for more hints of words to use at each step.

Getting ready

Step 1. Describe your mission as a vision of what might be.

Hint: Use positive words. Focus on the improvement you seek in love and justice. Draw on question 5 from the Activity 2 worksheet.

Step 2. Think of both who would respond to the vision and who would be the best helper – whether or not a religious person. Write in his or her name.

Hint: Think broadly. Draw on question 6 from the Activity 2 worksheet. Who is most able to help you? Don't exclude potential teammates who may not be religious. Choose anyone who is committed to love and justice as primary values. They already share in God's mission of love and justice even though they do not know it. If the person is religious (active, lapsed, or one who believes without belonging), go on to step 3. If the person's faith is unknown or you know already that the person is an agnostic (says it's impossible to know whether or not God exists) or an atheist (says there is no God), go on to step 3a through 6a.

Step 3. Write out or note how you will describe your mission in a way that would interest this person, and include a direct way to ask him or her to help. Note also an appropriate next step to take together.

Hint: Avoid overly religious language in this step. Draw on question 6 from the Activity 2 worksheet to speak naturally and simply about your mission in everyday language and put it in a way that would interest this particular person. Write out a simple and direct request for help to use if the prospective helper responds positively. If he or she agrees, note here an appropriate next step that you might take together. Your specific vision or mission will suggest what that step might be.

ACTIVITY 6: WORKSHEETS:
Finding a teammate

Step 4. Write out how, with permission, you might describe how you see that the mission can be part of God's mission.

Hint: Begin with asking for permission to share your belief and be ready to be brief. If the answer is "no," go on to step 6. If "yes," draw on your answer to question 7 of the Activity 2 worksheet. You are not trying to make a statement of faith or teach anyone. You are sharing what motivates you to carry on this mission – something your teammate has a right to know. Rely on the love and justice in your mission to provide the basis for connecting it with God's mission of love and justice and to talk of it as a mission; and make explicit reference to God, God's mission, your faith, the Bible, or the church.

Step 5. Write out how, with permission, you could share with your teammate how church life and worship help you to follow through on a mission; and wonder if he or she might find such help there too.

Hint: (If you are not a churchgoer, skip this step.) Ask for permission to share where you go for help. If "no," go on to step 6. If "yes," draw on your answer to question 8 on the Activity 2 worksheet. Note how church life and worship help you to follow through on a mission. Note also a way to invite your teammate to share how he or she might find help there in the same or some other way.

Doing it

Step 6. Go to the potential teammate, share the mission, and ask him or her to help you. If he or she agrees, perhaps, outline your next step together.

Hint: Draw on your answer to step 3 (above). Keep it simple and direct. Do ask for help. He or she can't respond if you don't ask. If the answer is "no," thank the other for considering it. Don't be discouraged; it may not be the right time for that person. Go on to find a person who will help you. If the answer is "yes," perhaps, share an appropriate next step for the two of you to take together. Make notes here that might help you.

Step 7. When the time is right, point to God's connection with the vision.

Hint: When the other shows interest or talks of some of the good results possible, ask for permission to share some of your thoughts about how the mission could be part of God's mission. Draw on your thinking from step 4 above. Make notes here that might help you.

ACTIVITY 6: WORKSHEETS:
Finding a teammate

Step 8. When the time is right, talk about church life and worship as places to go for help to follow through on the mission, and invite him or her to share how church life and worship might help him or her in the same or some other way.

Hint: (If you are not a churchgoer, omit this step.) Draw on your notes from step 5 above. Make notes here that might help you. Ask for permission to share what helps you that might help him or her too.

COMPLETE THE FOLLOWING FOR A POTENTIAL TEAMMATE WHO IS NOT RELIGIOUS OR WHOSE RELIGIOUS CONVICTIONS ARE UNKNOWN.

Step 3a. Adapting question 6 on your worksheet from Activity 2 for this mission field, restate the mission in a way that might appeal to this potential teammate. Include how you will ask for help, if the response is positive.

Hint: Be straightforward in sharing the mission. Invite questions to clarify it or how you expect to work for it at this point. Finally, have in mind a direct way to ask for help. For example, the postal worker wanting help to speak up to the manager about unfair work conditions might say: "When I do speak up, I need to check with someone afterwards to see how I came across. Could I come to you for that help?" If he or she agrees, note here an appropriate next step for you both.

Step 4a. Adapting the answer to question 7 on your Activity 2 worksheet, think of some way to express, with permission, how you see God might be connected with the mission. Use words that will interest the other person without being pretentious; are free of unnecessarily religious wording; and make explicit reference to God, God's mission, your faith, the Bible, or the church; and are a genuine sharing of a viewpoint and not a call to faith. Write them in here.

Hint: Note something like, "May I share something of what I believe about this?... I'm not asking you to share my belief, but rather, I suspect you might be interested – and you might want to know – some more about where I'm coming from." If the answer is yes, share the connection you see. Example from the postal worker: "I can't believe work is meant to be such a drag. According to Genesis, we are made to love and to work. So, there's hope we can make this place better for all of us – the boss included." If the answer is "no," go to step 6a.

Step 5a. Adapting question 8 from your Activity 2 worksheet, write out how you might point to church life and worship as places where you go for help to follow through; how he or she might find it helpful as well; and how you might offer to help him or her to explore the possibility. Be as free of religious language as possible.

Hint: Ask for permission: "Our goal is going to be hard to reach. May I share with you where I go for help when I need it?... It will be religious, but maybe you'd like to know how this works for me." If "no," go on to step 6a; if the going gets tough, the answer

ACTIVITY 6: WORKSHEETS:
Finding a teammate

might be "yes" later. Example from the postal worker: "I'll be brief. I find that when I pray, I get helped in unexpected ways, and when I stop praying the 'coincidences' stop happening. Church also holds up the values I want to live by and that helps me to keep going. It might help you, too. If you are curious for more, let me know."

Doing it

Step 6a. Go to the potential teammate, share the mission, and ask him or her to help you. If he or she agrees, outline your next step together.

Hint: Draw on your answer to step 3a (above). Keep it simple and direct. Do ask for help. He or she can't respond if you don't ask. If the answer is "no," thank the other for considering it. Don't be discouraged; it may not be the right time for that person. Go on to find a person who will help you. If he or she agrees to help, share an appropriate next step for the two of you to take together. Your specific vision or mission will suggest what that step might be.

Step 7a. If and when the time is right, try pointing to God's connection with the mission.

Hint: When the other person shows interest or talks of some of the good results possible, it may be time to ask for permission to share some of what you believe about the mission. Draw on your thinking from step 4a above. Make notes here that might help you.

Step 8a. If and when the time is right, talk about church life and worship as where you go for help to follow through on the mission; and how he or she might find it helpful as well; and offer to help him or her to explore that possibility.

Hint: Draw on your notes from step 5a above. Ask for permission to share what helps you that might help him or her too. Be sure to include something like "If you are curious for more, let me know." Make notes here that might help you.

Examples

Example A: Jim's and Margaret's missions on a specific day 13

Example B: Hints and sample responses for the home and work mission fields 19

Example C: My daily missions at a glance – two sample columns.. 25

Example D: Sample road map for my home and work mission fields 27

Example E: Finding a teammate at work 32

Example F: Finding a teammate – stories 33

Example G: A completed glance chart and road map 53

> We include here examples of Margaret's fully completed glance chart and road map so that you can see what they look like (see p. 14 for her daily missions). Refer to these charts for inspiration or guidance as you work on your own glance chart and road map.

Living the Gospel: A Guide for Individuals and Small Groups

EXAMPLE G:
A completed glance chart and road map

MARGARET'S DAILY MISSIONS AT A GLANCE

	HOME	WORK	COMMUNITY	WIDER WORLD	LEISURE	SPIRITUAL HEALTH	CHURCH LIFE AND OUTREACH
1. What has God been doing in this mission field? What message am I getting?	help my son and daughters	help my boss	help the homeless	help the poor	write for pleasure	I need to be fed	fulfill my role to help my son prepare for Confirmation
2. As I think about God's message, what is my vision or goal for this mission field?	talk with them about dating and drugs	pray about opinions to pass on to the boss	a shelter for the homeless	increase opportunities for the poor	write about our need for God	seek help from others and on my own	all of us talk about following Jesus
3. What am I doing right now to make this vision or goal a reality?	talking together openly and easily	doing effective work and offering sound ideas when asked	working to provide a shelter	getting informed on what can be done	writing about drawing others into following Jesus	fourth-day group and my own devotions	memorize creed and share about living the baptismal covenant
4. What do I still need to do?	help kids make the connection between faith and daily life	keep responding when asked	keep motivating the group so they don't give up	find specific ways to help	write a how-to course on drawing in new members	keep at both of these	continue the sharing after he is confirmed
5. What, specifically, will I do to make my vision or goal a reality? When will I do it?	tie my faith to what I say about dating and drugs this week	when next asked, to continue to think sensibly and to pray for help	share my own story next time it's needed	find three ways to help this month	start writing the course next week	continue to keep up with my fourth-day group and my own devotional activities	one of us shares at dinner tonight "what God's done in my life today"

Section IV 53

Living the Gospel: A Guide for Individuals and Small Groups

EXAMPLE G:
A completed glance chart and road map continued

MARGARET'S DAILY MISSIONS AT A GLANCE

	HOME	WORK	COMMUNITY	WIDER WORLD	LEISURE	SPIRITUAL HEALTH	CHURCH LIFE AND OUTREACH
6. Who can work with me to carry out this mission? How will I interest him or her?	my wise friend Molly – "help me to think through what I'll say"	trusted coworker Ellen – "keep me practical"	my group – "I believe the homeless are our neighbors"	Mary – "poor people need an equal chance"	Pastor – "will you be my critic?"	fourth-day group – "let's make our meetings make a difference"	son and daughters – "we can help each other"
7. How can I talk about being part of God's mission with my teammate?	"God's coworkers need physical and mental health"	"I trust I'll be led somehow"	"God cares; we care too"	"God must want equal chances for the poor"	"Jesus wants effective witnesses"	"help me be specific about how God helps me"	"God will help us to understand our baptismal vows"
8. How could I encourage my teammate to turn to the church for help and support?	"receiving communion will help us"	"praying helps me – it might help you"	"church tells me there's hope – it might help you to hope too"	"might help to hear church readings say God wants equal chances for everyone"	"prayer might help you to help me"	"I pray for help and it comes – might help you do the same"	"Church might help your believing and living"

54   Section IV

EXAMPLE G:

A completed glance chart and road map continued

MARGARET'S ROAD MAP OF HER DAILY MISSIONS

	VISION/GOAL (question 2 from Activity 3)	TEAMMATE (question 6 from Activity 3 – how to interest him or her)	MISSION (question 5 from Activity 3 – what to do or action/s to take and when to start)
HOME	talk with them about dating and drugs	my wise friend Molly – "help me to think through what I'll say"	tie my faith to what I say about dating and drugs this week
WORK	pray about opinions to pass on to the boss	trusted coworker Ellen – "keep me practical"	when next asked for help, to continue to think sensibly and to pray for help
COMMUNITY	a shelter for the homeless	my group – "I believe the homeless are our neighbors"	share my own story next time it's needed
WIDER WORLD	increase opportunities for the poor	Mary – "poor people need an equal chance"	find three ways to help this month
LEISURE	write about our need for God	pastor – "will you be my critic?"	start writing the course next week
SPIRITUAL HEALTH	seek help from others and on my own	fourth-day group – "let's make our meetings make a difference"	continue to keep up with my fourth-day group and my own devotional activities
CHURCH LIFE AND OUTREACH	all of us talk about following Jesus	son and daughters – "we can help each other"	one of us shares at dinner tonight "what God's done in my life today"

Tables

Table 1: The fields of daily life 15

Table 2: Enhancing responses to Activity 2 worksheets 23

Table 3: God's gifts to us 29

Table 4: A guide for Christian decision making 35

Resources

Resource A: Our fields of daily life are our daily mission fields

Our fields of daily life are really our daily mission fields. These are the places in life where we can act as Christ's agents or missionaries. How can we be sure that what we are doing is really God's work? Each action that you listed in Activity 1 (p. 38) probably possesses these five characteristics in one way or another and, so, qualifies as a mission.

1. A mission is centered in love and justice. The action in both deed and word is centered in love and justice. This is the most important characteristic. Will your mission improve the daily lives of people you are close to? Will it benefit people you don't even know? Remember, we love face-to-face, and, when we want to express love in public life, we do it by being just.

2. A mission is specific and, therefore, calls for specific actions in what you do and say. A possible mission might be to comfort a friend who has just lost a spouse by visiting and being ready to talk about God's presence to strengthen and guide us during these times. Another mission might be to support low-income housing in your neighborhood by speaking out that you believe that we are made as one human family and are called to care for all members of the family regardless of economic standing.

3. A mission costs you something. You spend yourself, your time, your energy, and your various resources to bring about something better. You are choosing to turn over your possessions and yourself to God's work. And risk is involved. Think of situations like the parent who risks a teen's anger to teach healthy, life-preserving values or the whistle-blowers who risk their jobs on behalf of honesty in business or government.

4. A mission can be carried out only with God's help. Our capacity to bring greater love and justice by ourselves is limited. By ourselves, we are even more limited in our capacity to help in broken or wrong situations. Further, the best of our intentions and actions can be infected with self-serving and self-righteousness. We always need God's help to keep us centered on the needs of others rather than on our own needs. This is why we say a mission can be carried out only with God's help.

5. A mission brings joy. You are sharing in God's work and seeing what you do bear fruit as love and justice grow. You'll have a sense of rightness about what you're doing – almost as if you're getting in line or realigned with God's priorities. Suppose, as your mission, you take on helping a friend who is undergoing cancer treatment. The help and comfort you offer are part of God's help and comfort. Your friend's gratitude makes you thank God for working through you. Another example might be when you see resistance decline as you speak-up for low-income housing in your community. Here, too, you trust and give thanks that this is God's work through you and not simply the impact of your own skills of persuasion. Such experiences have a very special kind of joy. Finally, when there seems to be little response or change in whatever you are doing, you will still have a joy – a peace "which surpasses understanding" (Phil. 4:7). You sense that God is with you and trust that God will overcome some day.

Missions change. As one is completed, a new one will take its place. You may also find yourself adjusting how you work on a particular mission. You may need to try several times before you are able to converse effectively with a hostile coworker. Consider his or her situation, pray about it, and take your cues from the leading of the Spirit. You may change your whole approach. As you sense being called to a new mission or to adjust an existing one, feel secure in making the change. God will give you the help you need.

The grand name for Christian work

You may be surprised to call what you are doing a "mission." You may see it as just helping out a buddy at work, or talking your daughter through a breakup, or helping an elderly widow find a better apartment, or writing a letter to the local newspaper supporting a candidate who works to protect the environment for future generations. These seemingly small things that we do every day really are missions, and not to say so robs these actions of their meaning. God's work is sacred even when it seems mundane. Any action that meets these five characteristics is a "mission:" it is loving and just, specific, costly, done only with God's help, and brings joy. Go beyond just playing golf with your friend when he's down. Ask God to give him what he needs and that your continuing presence and words will be part of God's help and healing. Your friendship can achieve so much more when you pray to be an instrument of God's care. Pray this way for all of your missions.

Beware of how the best of intentions – what you are tempted to call a "mission" – can be self-serving. You call on God for help with a friend and then you're tempted to expect something in return. Or you might overestimate your own ability to counsel your daughter and then be led to act or talk in ways that don't respect the complexity and range of the emotions she may be experiencing. Or you might recommend to a friend the first apartment that comes along so that you can stop showing your friend around. You need God's help to center on the other's needs rather than your own. Even the simplest of missions are carried out only with God's help. While your missions may never be done perfectly, you can be sure that they will be done better the more open you are to God's leading and help as you do them.

"Mission" carries the two-fold meaning of words as well as actions. Correcting wrongs calls for words as well as actions. Besides acting, we need to talk about what we believe God wants to be corrected, why God wants it corrected, and how God, through the church, might help us to correct it.

"Mission" is the grand name for Christian work. All Christian actions – large and small – that are acts and words of love and justice are grand actions and deserve to be called missions.

Resource B: Four steps to practice finding a teammate

Practice in finding a teammate can be a rich learning experience. Do the practice in trios. If you are working alone, find a partner and follow the same steps omitting the observer.

Step one: Each person has the appropriate Activity 6 worksheets in hand or nearby for reference as needed. As leader, clarify the process with a demonstration. Do this while the whole group is still together. Ask a trio to volunteer for the demonstration. Talk them through each part of steps Two, Three, and Four. In the actual practice, this trio plays out the other two situations and has extra time for reflection.

Step two: In each trio, decide who will be the first one to practice finding a teammate. Then choose someone to be the potential teammate. The one seeking a teammate, the "seeker," describes the potential teammate he or she has in mind. Give the name, sex, age, the characteristics that make the person a potential teammate, and any information about his or her religious convictions – that is, whether the seeker knows the potential teammate is a person of faith (active, lapsed, or one who believes without belonging), an agnostic (says it is impossible to know whether or not God exists), an atheist (says there is no God), or a person whose faith is not known. This gives the person taking the role of the potential teammate enough information to know how to act out the role. From that point on, the potential teammate acts the role as he or she chooses. The third person in the trio acts as an observer and looks for what helped or hindered the approach made. If there are four in the group, two act as observers.

Step three: Begin the practice and go as far, at least, as outlining the mission, asking for help with it, and working with the response from the potential teammate. Don't be surprised if the potential teammate asks for details about what he or she will be asked to do. Most people would. Also, be ready to share, if appropriate, a next step to take together. Keep in mind that the seeker's talk of how God might be present is optional and will probably be determined by what the seeker knows about the faith position of the potential teammate. Also optional is how church life helps the seeker to carry out his or her missions and how it might help the potential teammate. However, do try to include both of these options in the practice. This practice will probably take about five to eight minutes.

Step four: At the end of the practice, the observer will share what was seen to help or hinder the approach. Second, the potential teammate will share what he or she experienced. Third, the seeker will share what he or she experienced.

Now, switch roles and repeat the process until everyone has practiced finding a teammate. When possible, allow up to 20 minutes for each round. When all three have practiced, the trio will share various learnings and discuss them as desired. Enrich the sharing by pairing up trios for the reflection.

Moving Still Further Ahead

Recall the "member mission" vision: all members as agents of Jesus' mission to make every part of their daily lives more loving and more just; and their congregations guiding and empowering them through their common life and worship.

"Member mission" has been in formation since 1999. The research that provided for a book and guide was funded by Trinity Church grants. Excerpts from the book, *When the Members are the Missionaries* (2002), have been included in this guide – stories of people living their daily missions and how churches can support their members on mission. The book called for this guide which, we trust, helps people to connect the vision with their own daily lives.

Over these years, the experience and feedback from on-site training and consultations have provided for the continuous development and improvement of the process and its resources, including this guide.

Scores of churches with their hundreds of members in five denominations in the United States and ten communions in Tanzania suggest the breadth of our learning. Those "learnings" greatly shaped this present work.

Slightly condensed versions of this workbook are available in Spanish, Chinese, and Swahili (write to membermission@aol.com for copies).

Use the various parts of the guide to suit the needs of each user or group. We believe that each part of this guide can help people to rethink their daily activities to see how they can be – and often are – part of God's mission.